Merry Christmas

Adult Coloring Book

Oancea Camelia

Merry Christmas

Merry Christmas!

New adventures
to be had
New memories
to be made

Merry
Christmas

Merry Christmas!

Wishing
YOU
A VERY
MERRY
CHRISTMAS

have
a
JOLLY
CHRISTMAS

Merry Christmas

JOY TO THE WORLD

NOEL